ADVENTURES IN UNPLUGGED CODING

CODING
WITH
MYTHICAL CREATURES

BY KYLIE BURNS

Express!

BELLWETHER MEDIA • MINNEAPOLIS, MN

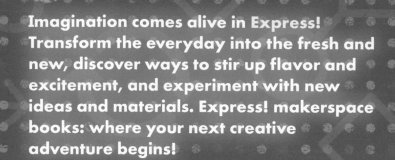

Express!

Imagination comes alive in Express!
Transform the everyday into the fresh and
new, discover ways to stir up flavor and
excitement, and experiment with new
ideas and materials. Express! makerspace
books: where your next creative
adventure begins!

This edition first published in 2024 by Bellwether Media, Inc.

No part of this publication may be reproduced in whole or in part without written permission of the publisher.
For information regarding permission, write to Bellwether Media, Inc., Attention: Permissions Department,
6012 Blue Circle Drive, Minnetonka, MN 55343.

Library of Congress Cataloging-in-Publication Data

Names: Burns, Kylie, author.
Title: Coding with mythical creatures / by Kylie Burns.
Description: Minneapolis, MN : Bellwether Media Inc., 2024. | Series: Express!. Adventures in unplugged coding |
  Includes bibliographical references and index. | Audience: Ages 7-13 | Audience: Grades 4-6 | Summary:
  "Information accompanies instructions for various mythical-creature-themed activities that demonstrate skills needed
  for coding. The text level and subject matter are intended for students in grades 3 through 8"-- Provided by publisher.
Identifiers: LCCN 2023021948 (print) | LCCN 2023021949 (ebook) | ISBN 9798886875140 (library binding) |
  ISBN 9798886875645 (paperback) | ISBN 9798886877021 (ebook)
Subjects: LCSH: Computer programming--Juvenile literature. | Animals, Mythical--Juvenile literature. | CYAC: Computer
  programming. | Mythical animals. | LCGFT: Activity books. | Instructional and educational works.
Classification: LCC QA76.6115 .B872 2024 (print) | LCC QA76.6115 (ebook) | DDC 005.13--dc23/eng/20230515
LC record available at https://lccn.loc.gov/2023021948
LC ebook record available at https://lccn.loc.gov/2023021949

Text copyright © 2024 by Bellwether Media, Inc. EXPRESS and associated logos are trademarks
and/or registered trademarks of Bellwether Media, Inc.

Editors: Sarah Eason and Christina Leaf
Illustrator: Eric Smith
Series Design: Brittany McIntosh
Graphic Designer: Paul Myerscough

Printed in the United States of America, North Mankato, MN.

TABLE OF CONTENTS _ □ X

Coding is a way of **communicating** with computers so they can carry out tasks. When you are told to do something, your brain receives the instruction. Because the instruction is in a language you understand, you can follow the steps to perform the task. Coding is a way to communicate instructions to a computer in a language that it understands called **code**.

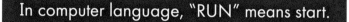

In computer language, "RUN" means start.

Unplugged coding activities involve following specific instructions through a series of steps, just like coding with a computer. But you do not need a computer to do these activities! In this book you will learn many awesome coding skills, such as **critical thinking**, through fun unplugged challenges with a **mythical** creatures theme.

LET'S GET STARTED!

HEY CERBERUS, FETCH! _ □ X

In coding, a **function** is a complete set of steps that create a specific action. By building a function, coders can create an event that occurs once each of the steps has been successfully completed by a computer.

YOU WILL NEED: _ □ X

- paper
- a pencil
- logical thinking

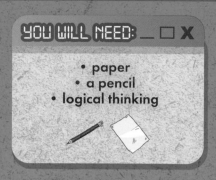

Try creating a function with this fun game. The steps on these pages are mixed up. Write them down in the most **logical** order to create a function that teaches Cerberus how to play fetch! Remember, logic is key!

LET'S GET STARTED!

Throw the toy a little farther. Repeat Steps 5 through 7 until Cerberus is a fetch pro!

Say "Go fetch!" and wait for Cerberus to bring you the toy.

Take Cerberus outside.

Throw the toy a short distance.

Wiggle the toy around to make Cerberus interested in playing.

When Cerberus returns, take back the toy.

DID YOU KNOW?

Functions are helpful because they can be used many times. When writing a program, a coder gives each function a name, such as "playfetch." When a coder wants an action to take place, they can insert the name of the function. This is easier than including a long list of steps and makes the code shorter!

Introduce the fetch toy.

TURN THE PAGE TO SEE HOW YOU DID!

Did you find it easy or difficult to order the steps to create the function? Take a look at the steps as they are shown in their correct order. Did you order them correctly? Coders must think of every single step before creating a function. If a step is out of order or missing, the function will not work.

1 Take Cerberus outside.

2 Introduce the fetch toy.

3 Wiggle the toy around to make Cerberus interested in playing.

4 Throw the toy a short distance.

5 Say "Go fetch!" and wait for Cerberus to bring you the toy.

6 When Cerberus returns, take back the toy.

7 Throw the toy a little farther. Repeat Steps 5 through 7 until Cerberus is a fetch pro!

HERE'S A TIP!

Start with the final goal and work backward to the beginning to make sure you do not miss a step. Then test out your function.

CODING CHALLENGE!   _ □ X

Try creating your own function. Think of a daily task and write down in order the steps you take to complete it. Then, ask a friend to follow the steps in your function to see if it works. Try a "washhands" function or a "tieshoes" function. To make it even more challenging, why not create a function for an obstacle course in your backyard?

GNOME CODER

In coding, a **value** represents information in a program that can change, like the score of a game. Values are stored within a **variable**, which acts as a container for information in a program. Each variable has a name and holds a specific type of value. An example of a variable can be "the number of fairies spotted today." The value could be represented by any number, such as 2, 5, 10, or 100.

In this activity, you will follow steps to draw five gnomes. Then you will use variables and values to color the gnomes. Roll the die to assign a value, or color, to each variable, or piece of clothing. Try it out!

YOU WILL NEED:

- a pencil
- paper
- colored pencils
- a six-sided die

LET'S COLOR SOME GNOMES!

1 Draw a U shape for the gnome's face.

2 Draw the gnome's nose and a mustache.

3 Add a beard, eyes, and eyebrows.

4

Draw a cone-shaped hat and two ears.

5

Draw a body with arms, hands, legs, and feet.

6

Add a shirt and pants. The bottom of the shirt can be jagged or straight.

7

Add a belt, shirt buttons, and shoes. Repeat the steps to make five gnomes.

8

Roll the die six times for each gnome, using the values to color each piece of clothing. Start with the first gnome, coloring each piece of clothing according to the chart below. Then do the same for the other gnomes. Color the clothing variables in order from head to toe, as follows:
hat, shirt, buttons, belt, pants, shoes

Roll:						
Use this color value:	blue	green	red	yellow	orange	purple

TURN THE PAGE TO COMPARE RESULTS!

Check out how our gnomes turned out below! Cute, huh?! How did your gnomes turn out? Did you have any repeated colors? Can you think of other ways to use variables and values to decide the colors for your gnomes?

DID YOU KNOW?

Some values are numbers. Others are represented by letters and words, or they can be true or false.

HERE'S A TIP!

Pretend you are walking home through a dark forest. In coding, you might write a variable called "I am in danger" that has either a "true" or "false" value. If you turn the corner and run into a dragon, then the value is "true," and you are in danger! But if you turn the corner and see nothing, the value is "false," and you can return home, safe and sound.

CODING CHALLENGE!   _ □ X

Try this activity another way with a friend, using a different set of values. This time, roll the die and think of six ways you could set values for the variable "types of snacks to eat." For each number, write down a different value, or snack! A roll of 1 could be popcorn, 2 could be cookies, and so on! Which snack do you want?

MINOTAUR MAZE _ □ X

Many coding problems can be solved faster by getting rid of steps that are not needed. This is called **optimization**. It is useful because it reduces the amount of **memory** a computer must use. Try out this fun maze activity to see optimization in practice.

YOU WILL NEED: _ □ X

- tracing paper
- a pencil
- to watch out!

In this activity, you have accidentally walked into an underground maze with many paths. It is the maze of the **Minotaur**! You must find the optimized path to escape the maze, and the Minotaur, who is right behind you!

LET'S GET OUT OF HERE!

TURN THE PAGE
TO SEE HOW YOU DID!

DID YOU KNOW?

Using fewer lines of code means a program runs more quickly and smoothly.

15

How did you optimize your escape route? Did you ask yourself what steps would take you through the maze fastest? Did you manage to find the optimized route on the first try, or did you have to go back and retrace your steps to find the best path? Check it out below!

EXIT

ENTRANCE

HERE'S A TIP!

Sometimes, coders need to ask questions to find the best way to optimize a code. They may ask, "What if I combined these steps?" or, "How can I remove steps that are slowing down the program?" These types of questions can help optimize the code.

CODING CHALLENGE!   _ □ X

With a friend, play this number-guessing game.

1. The first player chooses a secret number between 1 and 100 and writes it on a piece of paper.
2. The second player asks questions that will optimize finding the correct number. These must be questions that can be answered with yes or no. Consider if there are questions that can optimize the process, such as getting rid of a whole group of numbers with just one question.
3. Record on paper the number of questions asked. When the secret number has been correctly guessed, count how many questions it took to find it.
4. Switch roles and play again. The person with the fewest number of questions wins!

MEMORIZE THE MYTH! _ □ X

This activity focuses on critical thinking. Critical thinking involves creative solutions to tricky problems. Noticing patterns and organizing information into groups are two ways that coders think critically when they need to solve a problem.

Test your critical thinking skills with this mythical memory game. Be sure to read all the steps before beginning this activity.

YOU WILL NEED: _ □ X

- a timer
- paper
- a pencil
- logic and a good memory!

LET'S GET STARTED!

1
Set your timer for 30 seconds.

2
Press start on the timer.

3 Study the objects in the box below for exactly 30 seconds.

4 Close the book as soon as the time is up.

5 Write down or draw as many of the objects as you can remember.

TURN THE PAGE TO SEE HOW YOU DID!

DID YOU KNOW?

A coder notices the little details. When coders run into problems, they think critically by testing, repeating the process, and thinking it through until they find a solution.

Did your critical thinking skills help you remember the items in the picture? Check them out again below. Did you get all of them? If not, how many did you get? What critical thinking tricks did you use to help you remember them?

HERE'S A TIP!

Here are some more critical thinking tricks to help you organize and remember information. When grouping things, look for similarities, such as colors or shapes, to help you. For example, group red objects or round objects. You can also group objects by type, such as animals or toys.

CODING CHALLENGE!

_ □ X

Try this next challenge to practice more critical thinking skills.

You Will Need:

- a friend
- a tray or cookie sheet
- a dish towel
- a timer, set for 30 seconds
- a range of small objects
- a pen
- paper

1. Ask your friend to leave the room so they cannot see what you are doing.
2. Choose 5 to 10 different small objects and arrange them on the tray.
3. Cover the tray with a dish towel, and then ask your friend to join you.
4. Remove the towel and start the timer. Your friend has 30 seconds to memorize the items.
5. Replace the towel. Now, ask your friend what was on the tray. Write down their answers. How did they do?
6. Swap places and test out your memory by repeating Steps 1 through 5.
7. The player who correctly remembers the most items wins!

I HOPE YOU ENJOYED UNPLUGGED CODING!

GLOSSARY

code—instructions for a computer

communicating—sharing knowledge or information

critical thinking—a way of thinking that involves breaking down a problem or information and results in a logical conclusion

function—a part of a code that can be used over and over

logical—related to thinking that is based on facts or reason

memory—the electronic storing of information in a computer

Minotaur—a monster in Greek myths that is half man and half bull

mythical—related to myths; myths are stories or ideas from a certain group or culture.

optimization—a way to improve a code so that it works more quickly and takes up less space in a computer

value—a piece of information in a code; values are often part of a variable.

variable—part of a code that stores information; variables contain related values.

TO LEARN MORE ___ □ X

AT THE LIBRARY

Lang, Taylor. *Critical Thinking Activities for Kids.* Emeryville, Calif.: Rockridge Press, 2021.

McCue, Camille. *Getting Started with Coding: Get Creative with Code!* Indianapolis, Ind.: John Wiley and Sons, 2019.

Prottsman, Kiki. *How to Be a Coder.* New York, N.Y.: DK Publishing, 2019.

ON THE WEB

FACTSURFER

Factsurfer.com gives you a safe, fun way to find more information.

1. Go to www.factsurfer.com.

2. Enter "coding with mythical creatures" into the search box and click 🔍 .

3. Select your book cover to see a list of related content.

INDEX

_ □ X